DATE			

SUPERBIKES

THE HISTORY OF MOTORCYCLES

Peter Lafferty and David Jefferis

Franklin Watts

New York London Toronto Sydney

Illustrated by
Chris Forsey
Terry Hadler
Ron Jobson
Michael Roffe

Photographs supplied by
Alan Cathcart
David Jefferis
Don Morley

Technical consultant
Patrick Devereux

© 1990 Franklin Watts

Franklin Watts Inc.
387 Park Avenue South
New York, NY 10016

Printed in Belgium

Library of Congress Cataloging-in-Publication Data

Lafferty, Peter.
Superbikes : the story of motorcycles / Peter Lafferty and David Jefferis.
p. cm. –– (Wheels)
Summary: Surveys the history and functions of motorcycles, from their invention in the 1850s to their wartime uses and present sporting capabilities.
ISBN 0–531–14039–3
1. Motorcycles—Juvenile literature. [1. Motorcycles.]
I. Jefferis. David. II. Title.
TL440.L34 1990
629.227'5—dc20   89–29307
                                  CIP
                                  AC

SUPERBIKES

Contents

Introduction	4
Red hot steamers	6
Motorcycle pioneers	8
Curtiss, the beach rider	10
War on two wheels	12
The golden age of biking	14
The story of Harley-Davidson	16
Tidal wave from Japan	18
Champion!	20
Off-roading	22
Future bike	24
Superbike century	26
Facts and records	28
Bike technology	30
Index	32

Introduction

Superbikes are the biggest and fastest motorcycles. A powerful superbike like the Kawasaki ZZ-R1100 can accelerate from 0 to 100 km/h (62 mph) in less than four seconds.

The word superbike dates back to the late 1960s, when the Triumph Trident and BSA Rocket III were introduced. Both bikes combined high power with safe handling to make them, for a while, the leaders of the pack.

Bikes like these evolved from attempts in the 1800s to attach motors to bicycles. At first, steam engines were used, but these machines were not very successful. Then, in the 1880s, the gasoline engine was invented. It produced high power for its weight and became the type of engine used ever since.

The layout of the motorcycle has not changed much since the pioneer Werner brothers fitted an engine between the wheels of their 1901 machine. Today's bikes follow much the same pattern. Most bikes have a chain to link the engine and gearbox to the rear wheel. Some makers, such as BMW, use a shaft to transfer power to the back wheel. This is easier to maintain, but for sheer efficiency on a powerful bike, a chain is still the best.

Superbikes are almost all equipped with powerful front and rear disc brakes. Some have antilock systems fitted to reduce the risk of a dangerous skid on wet or greasy roads. Streamlined bodywork is now standard too, keeping most of the wind blast off a rider's body. Styling usually comes before function though – very few machines have a wide enough fairing, or bodywork, to keep your hands dry when it's raining!

▷ The Triumph Trident, a superbike of the 1960s, is now a motorcycle classic. Both this bike and the BSA Rocket III had three-cylinder engines, unusual then and now.

Motorcycles old and new

These two bikes cover 75 years of motorcycling. The 1914 Indian Hendee Special was an advanced machine for its time and was the first bike to have an electric starter. The layout is similar to a modern bike, though detail differences include the swept back handlebars and low-set saddle. Indian was once the biggest motorcycle maker in the world. Sadly, it stopped making bikes in the 1950s.

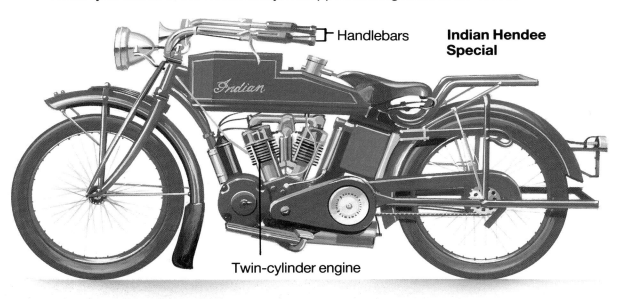

Handlebars

Indian Hendee Special

Twin-cylinder engine

The 1989 Yamaha OW01 FZR 750R is about as close as you can come to a "street-legal" racing bike. As superbikes go, it is quite light – 187 kg (411 lb) before fuel, oil and rider. Many big bikes weigh in with an extra 50 kg (110 lb) or more. The Yamaha's light weight, together with a rigid frame and powerful brakes, make for excellent handling and roadholding.

Yamaha OW01

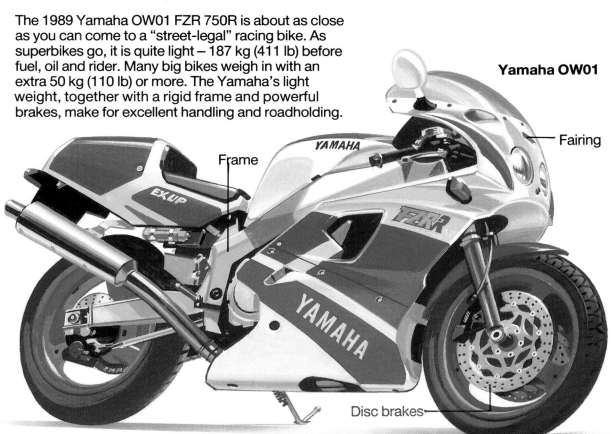

Fairing

Frame

Disc brakes

Red hot steamers

The first motorbikes were simply powered bicycles. In the 1850s, cycling was a popular sport and a means of getting around.

In 1869, the French brothers Ernest and Pierre Michaux attached a small steam engine to a "bone-shaker" bicycle. A belt from the steam engine drove the bike's back wheel. The machine was not very powerful, but it managed a 16 km (10 mile) spin from the Michaux garage in Paris to the small town of St. Germain-en-Laye. The Michaux steamer never became popular though, perhaps because the rider had to sit directly over the engine's boiler!

Other inventors also built steam powered bicycles. One of the most successful was the machine made by American engineer Lucius Copeland. In 1885 he fixed a steam engine to a penny-farthing bicycle. The engine drove the huge rear wheel. Copeland's steamer machine could manage a speed of 20 km/h (12 mph) on level ground. It was quite reliable, completing a 192 km (120 miles) journey without trouble.

Copeland set up a company to make lots more of the steam-powered cycles. Unfortunately he ran into severe financial problems and had to close his factory in 1890.

◁ Apart from their steam power experiments, the Michaux brothers made a number of bicycle design improvements. Pierre Michaux had the simple idea of attaching pedals directly to the front wheel, much better than the stirrup foot levers in use at the time. Michaux bicycles were popular – there was even a Michaux Club in New York.

▽ Other 19th century steamers included this three-wheel model. The von Saurbronne-Davis velocipede had a gasoline powered steam engine. A hand wheel was used to steer and the rider sat on a padded seat.

△ Though they looked dangerous, penny-farthings were easy to ride, once you learned the art of climbing aboard. Copeland's machine had its small wheel at the front, an arrangement designed for safe braking.

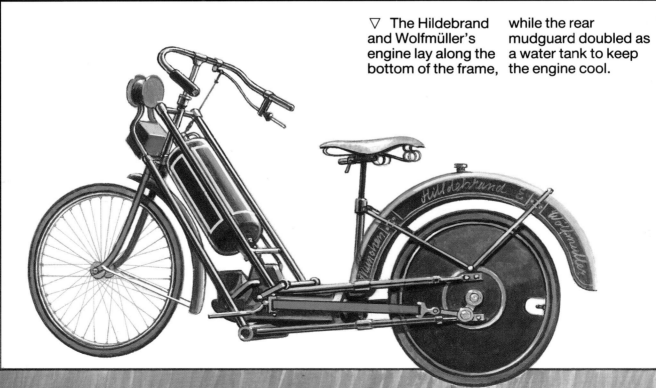

▽ The Hildebrand and Wolfmüller's engine lay along the bottom of the frame, while the rear mudguard doubled as a water tank to keep the engine cool.

Motorcycle pioneers

round 1876, German engineer Nikolaus Otto built an internal combustion engine, so-called because fuel was burned inside it. Otto's engine design gave more power for its weight than other types of engine. The internal combustion engine has been very successful; in various forms it has propelled most kinds of transportation, including cars, trucks and motorcycles.

In 1885, Karl Benz developed a lightweight version of Otto's engine for his first car, a spindly three-wheel contraption. In the same year two other Germans, Gottleib Daimler and Wilhelm Maybach, put a Benz-type engine into a wooden cycle frame. Daimler's 17-year-old son Paul rode this first motorcycle 17 km (10 miles) around the town of Cannstatt. It is said that during the ride, the saddle burst into smoldering flames because it was so close to the hot, gasoline fueled engine!

Nine years later, in Munich, Heinrich and Wilhelm Hildebrand joined in partnership with Alois Wolfmüller to build a twin-cylinder motorcycle. This became the first commercially produced motorbike and over 1000 were built in the first two years of production.

Factories were based in Munich but the exact number of bikes made is not known. Unfortunately, buyers found the Hildebrand and Wolfmüller unreliable. Sales soon dropped off and production stopped in 1897.

The bike held the record for its huge engine for many years. Only the current 1520 cc Honda Gold Wing has a bigger engine.

◁ △ The Daimler and Maybach machine had an extra wheel mounted on each side to keep it upright. These small wheels would have caused problems when cornering at high speed.

▷ Early bike designers couldn't decide where to put the engine, and many places were tried. In one instance an engine was mounted on a trolley towed behind the bike. The 1901 Werner was the first production bike with an engine between the wheels.

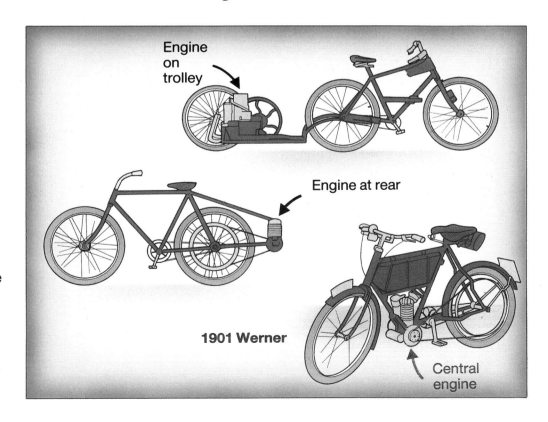

Engine on trolley

Engine at rear

1901 Werner

Central engine

Curtiss, the beach rider

Daimler and Maybach's motorcycle could manage a top speed of 19 km/h (12 mph). But as more efficient and powerful engines were developed, speeds rose dramatically. By 1900, short distance bursts of 144 km/h (90 mph) had been recorded. The bikes used in these record breaking dashes were often large and usually unsuited for normal road work.

One early speedster was American Glenn Curtiss. He was a pioneer airman who attacked the motorcycle speed record in 1907. The Curtiss machine had an eight-cylinder engine intended to power an aircraft, but installed on the bike for testing.

Curtiss unleashed his machine on a long stretch of sand at Ormond Beach, Florida. He had to ride along a measured "flying mile," the 1.6 km distance used for all speed record attempts, with space allowed at either end for starting and stopping. With his bike bucking and weaving on the uneven sand, Curtiss blasted through the mile in 26.4 seconds, to record a speed of 220 km/h (136 mph).

The motorcycle world was astonished and many people did not believe Curtiss could have reached this speed. He was accused of cheating and the record was never officially recognized. It was not until 1930 that the official record bettered the 1907 Florida run of Glenn Curtiss. Record attempts these days are carefully observed, with split-second timing calculated by computer.

Glenn Curtiss hurtles along Ormond Beach at over 200 km/h (125 mph). By modern standards early riders had little protection. Curtiss wore goggles, leather cap and leggings. A modern rider wears fireproof clothes, a full-length leather suit, and a crash helmet.

As speeds rose, bikes were enclosed in streamlined bodyshells to combat the effects of air drag. In 1937, BMW rider Ernst Henne rode one of the first streamliners to set a 279.5 km/h (173 mph) speed that stayed a record for 14 years.

△ Today's motorcycle speed record is held by American Donald Vesco and his streamliner bike *Lightning Bolt*. The record run was made on August 28, 1978, starting with a tow from a truck until *Lightning Bolt* was moving fast enough to stay upright. Vesco flicked a switch to retract two small balancer skids, then accelerated down a specially graded 17 km (10.6 mile) track, smoothed out of the rough surface of Bonneville Salt Flats in Utah. With its two Kawasaki engines howling, *Lightning Bolt* scorched down the line marked on the salt surface. After the speed runs, computers calculated the average speed. A new record – 512.733 km/h (318.598 mph)!

War on two wheels

When World War I broke out in 1914, motorcycles were put into service by the armed forces of the fighting powers.

Motorbikes were especially useful for carrying messages. At the time, radio was still being developed and was often unreliable for general use. Telephone lines were easily cut by enemy gunfire. So an important means of communication behind the lines was by car or motorcycle. Two-wheelers were often better than bigger vehicles since they could be ridden along roads blasted by shell craters and slimy with mud, where carts or trucks would get stuck.

Motorcycles were also fitted with sidecars and armed with powerful machine guns. Sidecar outfits were also useful as mini ambulances, each carrying a patient on a stretcher.

Later, in World War II, motorbikes were used to help spearhead Germany's high-speed motorized ground attacks. Together with tanks and troops, the bikes punched through enemy defense lines. Zundapps and BMWs were among the best bikes, and armed sidecar outfits were used in every battle area, from the hot deserts of North Africa to the chilly wastelands of Russia. In fact, the BMWs so impressed the Russians that they copied the design for their own armies after the war ended.

Other battle bikes included "flying flea" designs. These were miniature bikes made for parachute drops by airborne troops. After the war, an American flying flea minibike was sold as a runabout for lazy golf enthusiasts!

△ Mud and more mud was a feature of the battle lines in France during World War I, especially during the winter months. In this battle scarred landscape, motorcycle machine gunners guard a crossroads. An ambulance outfit takes a wounded soldier to a temporary hospital.

▷ Loaded up with soldiers, baggage, guns and ammunition, a World War II BMW R75 could reach nearly 90 km/h (55 mph) on reasonable roads.

Motorbikes were used by all the fighting powers, in every area of battle. The 300,000 bikes used by the Americans were mostly V-twins, so-called because the engine's two cylinders were arranged in a V-shape. British bikes included experimental Nortons with mortar-firing attachments.

The golden age of biking

After the end of World War I in 1918, motorcycling boomed. There was a huge demand for any kind of transportation, and many new bike makers started up in the 1920s.

Most motorbikes followed fairly similar layouts. A unique design was the 1921 Megola from Germany. It had a rotary engine, like a smaller version of those which had powered fighter planes in the war. Megola's engine was mounted on the front wheel, spinning faster than the wheel itself once under way! Nearly 2000 were made.

Racing and record breaking were popular with manufacturers, riders, newspapers and the public. The first

△ This is a Megola tourer, complete with bucket seat. Sports models had saddles.

▽ The Brough Superior was the Rolls-Royce of motorcycles. It had quality, power and speed. All were guaranteed by the makers to be able to hit 160 km/h (100 mph). Many famous riders rode them, including Lawrence of Arabia, who owned eight before being killed in a crash while riding one.

official speed record for motorcycles was set by American Ernie Walker on April 14, 1920. Riding a 994 cc Indian on the beach at Daytona, Florida, he hit 167.7 km/h (104.1 mph). This was far slower than the speed claimed by Glenn Curtiss 13 years before, but accurate timekeeping allowed it a place in the record books.

Motorcycling became the sport of kings when King Albert of Belgium learned to ride. By 1925 he was on his fifth machine, a fast Belgian Jeecy-Vea.

After the boom years of the "roaring twenties," the world depression of the 1930s resulted in most of the small bike makers going bust or being taken over when their markets collapsed. Without enough buyers, small companies did not have enough money in the bank to survive for long.

Names from the past

Of the hundreds of 1920s motorcycle makers, only a few remain in business today. Of the names shown below, only BMW has survived in anything like its original form. Though only a few dozen world-class manufacturers make bikes today, there are many small specialist firms which provide frames, engines or extra equipment.

△ Henderson bikes were first made in 1912. For a time, this was the most popular make in the United States.

▽ Scott's first bike went on sale in 1908. Scott machines had much racing success until the mid 1920s.

△ Indian was among the first to make a V-twin engine.

A starter motor was another Indian introduction.

△ Velocette started in 1904 and survived into the 1960s. Its Thruxton racer could top 192 km/h (120 mph).

▷ BMW launched its first shaft-drive bike in 1923.

The story of Harley-Davidson

Harley-Davidson bikes are big, heavy and reliable. The biggest Harleys, known as "hogs," are a favorite with police forces and motorcyclists of all types. The firm is an old one, a survivor from the earliest days of motorcycling.

In 1903 William Harley and Arthur Davidson built their first machine in a small shed near Davidson's home in Milwaukee, Wisconsin. It ran well, but had a top speed of just 40 km/h (25 mph).

They built a second, more powerful and rugged machine, which became known as the "silent gray fellow."

In 1908, a Harley-Davidson bike was entered in a two-day endurance race. By the end of the first day, half the 85 competitors had dropped out, defeated by the steep hills and bad roads. Arthur Davidson's brother, Walter, rode his bike to finish with a perfect 1000 points. The race committee was so impressed that Davidson was given an extra five

▷ Harley-Davidsons are best used for relaxed highway cruising. An Electra Glide like this weighs 370 kg (814 lb) even before you add the weight of the rider! An enthusiastic owner can add personal luxuries such as a stereo system.

points, making his score 1005 out of 1000!

In the 1960s and 1970s, Harley-Davidson ran into deep trouble. Japanese bikes were taking over much of the world market and introducing cheaply priced Harley look-alike bikes. Bad management at Harley resulted in bikes that were poorly developed and shoddily made. However, in 1981, new owners took over the company and have since put quality back into the bikes. Today's Harley-Davidsons are as reliable as the 1908 endurance racer.

△ This 1200 cc Harley was ridden by British rider Freddie Dixon in 1923 to break the Flying Kilometer record. His speed was a scorching 174 km/h (108.6 mph).

Highway cruisers

The look and style of the big Harley-Davidsons has inspired other makers to produce their own versions of the hog. The Italian Moto Guzzi California III has nearly as much chrome as its American cousin. The California was first introduced in 1975, and is still going strong. The Yamaha Virago has lots of chrome, laid-back handlebars and easy-rider styling to look similar to the specially-made custom bikes built by enthusiasts.

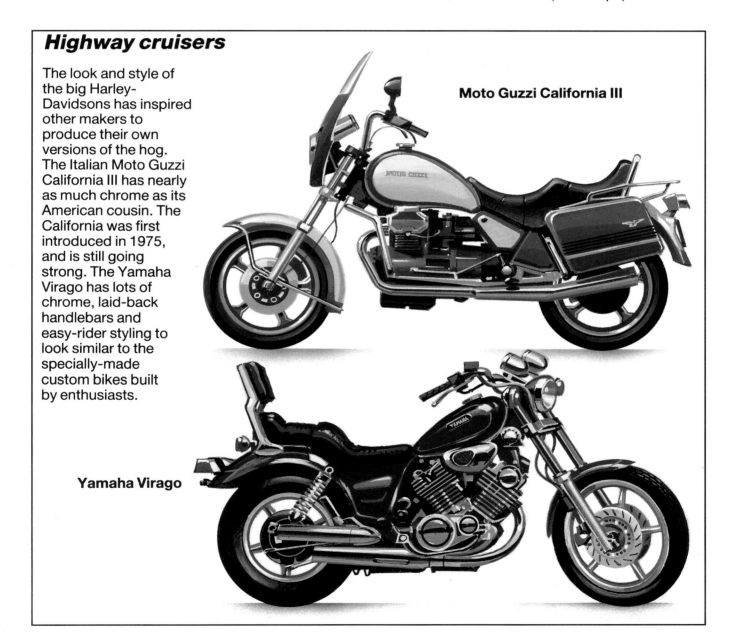

Moto Guzzi California III

Yamaha Virago

Tidal wave from Japan

In the 1950s, practically all the world's motorcycles were made by the British, Italians, Germans and Americans. However, instead of putting money into new bikes and factories many makers simply made small improvements to their existing models.

The first Japanese motorbikes hit world markets in the early 1950s. They were small, cheap and reliable. Despite the large sales of these new bikes, the European makers did not think they were much of a threat to the world of "big bikes." Then Honda entered a team for the 1959 Tourist Trophy race on the Isle of Man. They were not successful, but the following year, Honda bikes smashed the opposition.

Within a few years, Japanese makers had taken over most of the world's motorcycle markets from the traditional firms. The secret of their success was price, reliability and fast technical development.

The Honda CB750 of 1969 was the first Japanese superbike. It sold like hot cakes and was the final stage in the tidal wave of new models from Japan. Having swamped the market with small bikes, Japanese makers now showed they could make bikes as good as those of makers like Triumph or BMW.

Since then, Japanese makers have led the world in motorcycle design, though the Europeans and Americans have fought back. Italian, German, Spanish, British and American bikes are still made, though in small numbers compared to the millions of Japanese bikes produced each year.

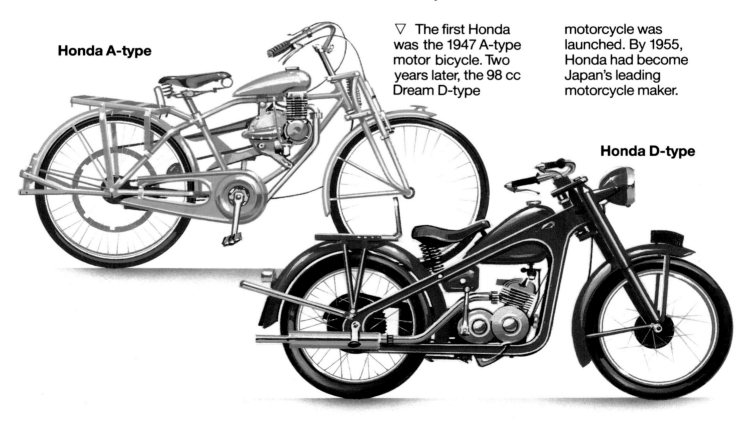

Honda A-type

▽ The first Honda was the 1947 A-type motor bicycle. Two years later, the 98 cc Dream D-type motorcycle was launched. By 1955, Honda had become Japan's leading motorcycle maker.

Honda D-type

△ In the 1970s there was a technical race between the Japanese makers for the biggest, fastest and most complex bike on the market. The Honda CBX, shown above, and the Kawasaki Z1300 were the high points, both having six cylinder engines. By today's standards, these bikes are heavy and slow-handling dinosaurs. Even so, they are now collector's items.

◁ Logos of the big four Japanese firms, painted on their machines.

19

Champion!

△ Riders lean over at alarming angles when cornering. Knees are protected with patches.

Each year motorcycle riders compete in Grand Prix races to decide who is world champion.

Grand Prix (French for "Big Prize") races are held at circuits around the world. Points are scored in each race, ranging from 20 points for the winner to 17 points for second place and down to just one point for 15th position. The rider with the most points at the season's end becomes champion. In a tie, the rider with most wins gets the championship.

Champion of champions was Giacomo Agostini of Italy. Between 1965 and 1976 he won a spectacular 122 Grand Prix races. He was world champion 15 times, seven times riding 350 cc bikes, eight on 500 cc machines.

There are various classes of race, depending on engine size, ranging from 80 cc up to the top class, 500 cc. Sidecar outfits compete in their own events. One of the earliest races was the Tourist Trophy, speeding along the twisting roads of the Isle of Man. In 1907, the 59 km (37 mile) race was won at an average speed of less than 65 km/h (41 mph). Today's racers blast around the same course at speeds of 193 km/h (120 mph) or more.

Motorcycle racing is very expensive, and most teams survive by getting sponsorship. In return for their money or free equipment, firms are allowed to advertise on the bikes and get publicity. People interested in sponsoring bike racing vary enormously, from tire companies to insurance firms.

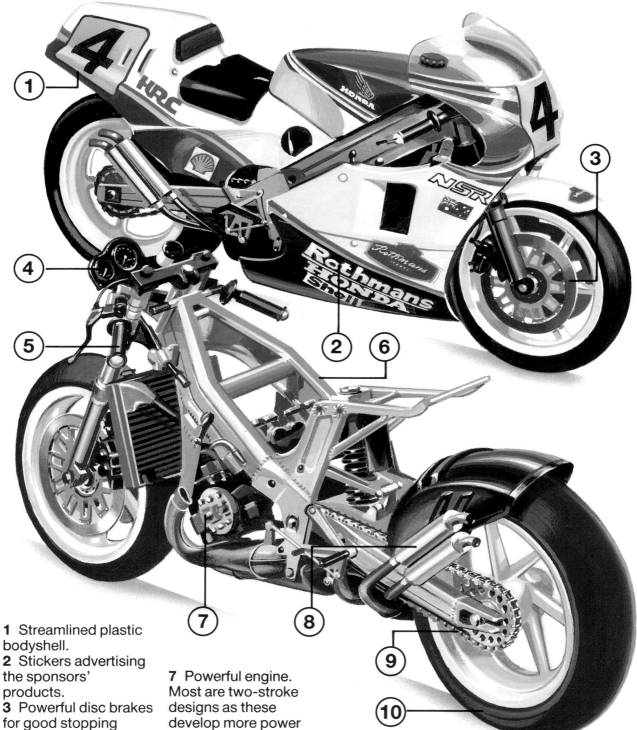

1 Streamlined plastic bodyshell.

2 Stickers advertising the sponsors' products.

3 Powerful disc brakes for good stopping power.

4 Instrument cluster.

5 Low set bars allow rider to crouch on bike to reduce air drag.

6 Strong, lightweight aluminum frame.

7 Powerful engine. Most are two-stroke designs as these develop more power for their weight than four-stroke engines (see page 30).

8 "Tin-can" exhaust, designed for power boosting rather than noise reduction!

9 Chain drive. Transmits more power than a shaft.

10 Dry weather "slick" tire has no tread pattern.

Off-roading

Competing with Grand Prix races for spectator support are a huge range of off-road bike sports. Trials events go back to the 1920s. They involve riding over rough terrain without losing control or putting a foot on the ground. Motocross races are held on dirt tracks, while enduros are long distance events. In an enduro, you get penalized for completing a section late. You also get points deducted for arriving early! Riders carry tools since any running repairs have to be done on the spot.

Like motocrossers, enduro bikes have tough knobby tires and beefed-up suspensions to cope with the bumps, rocks, mud and dirt of a typical event. One of the longest enduros was the 1988 Wynn's Safari, held across 10,000 km (6,200 miles) of Australia, from outback tracks to swamp bogs.

Among the dangers for one of the riders was the large rock he hit at 104 km/h (65 mph). In the outback, dust fills up most of the potholes, making them nearly invisible. Riding into one is bad enough, but when there's a rock at the bottom, you've got big trouble. Luckily the rider had no broken bones, but he spent an hour repairing the wheel enough to ride 64 km (40 miles) to a farm, where a farmer helped him weld it together. The next day he had a puncture – only to see a television helicopter hovering overhead, putting his plight on video!

The 1988 Safari was a tough event. Of the 77 bikes that entered, only 29 staggered in to the finish line.

▷ Enduro riders roar across the outback desert of Australia. Television crews filmed every hour of the race. Each night racers rested in special camps, while mechanics worked on the bikes. Flying doctors flew the injured to hospitals.

Another long enduro is the Paris-Dakar rally, which tracks across southern Europe and north Africa. It lasts three weeks and has long compass-navigation sections where people can easily get lost.

△ Motocross is a popular sport, especially good to watch as, unlike Grand Prix racing, you can usually stand a short distance from the action.

◁ MX and Enduro bike styles have been copied for street bikes. "Enduro replicas" are highly suited to potholed streets.

Future bike

The design of the superbike of the future will be shaped as much by safety and pollution concerns as by technical improvements.

Motorbikes are regarded as highly dangerous by many people, and few can argue that riding a bike is safer than driving a car. But bikes are a cheap way of getting around and avoiding congestion in cities – motorcycle messengers and cyclists can move through major cities in far less time than car or truck drivers.

Already motorcycle makers limit the power of their bigger engines, either because of strict laws, as in Japan, or voluntarily as with BMW's K1 bike. In fact, speed alone is rarely a killer, and proper rider training is more important than power limits. Canadian studies have proved that engine size is not a major factor in motorcycle accidents.

Antilock brakes, at present available on a few superbikes, may become widely used. Such brakes improve safety by preventing tire skids in slippery conditions. An antilock system senses when a wheel is about to lock, and relaxes the brake pressure slightly to compensate. In use, the antilock system is felt through the brake lever as a rapid pulsing action.

Another sensible design change already underway is the development of engines which run on lead-free fuel and use catalytic converters to remove most of the polluting gases from exhaust fumes.

Another feature of tomorrow's bikes will be lightweight construction. Aluminum frames with plastic bodies will be standard, as lightweight design improves fuel consumption.

◁ Traffic planners ought to be encouraging people to ride bicycles and motorcycles in cities as they cause less congestion than cars.

This Swiss Powa El-Tox is a design for a non-polluting electric city bike. As planned, the El-Tox will have a 50 km (31 mile) range on an overnight charge from the main electricity supply.

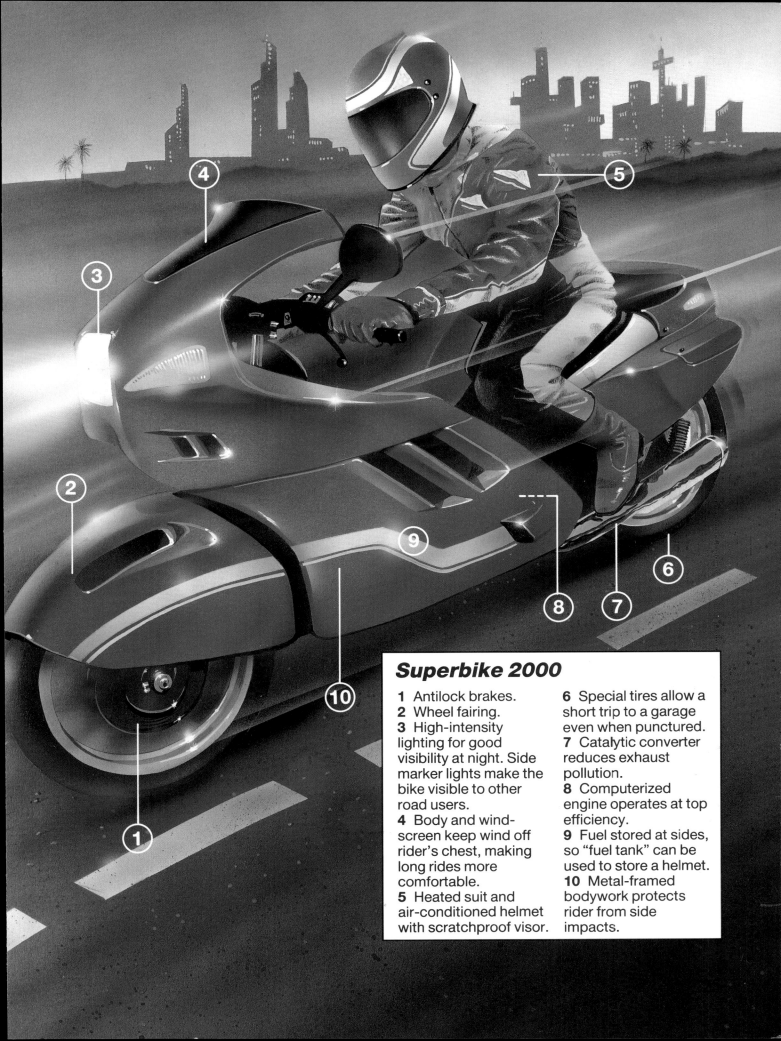

Superbike 2000

1 Antilock brakes.

2 Wheel fairing.

3 High-intensity lighting for good visibility at night. Side marker lights make the bike visible to other road users.

4 Body and windscreen keep wind off rider's chest, making long rides more comfortable.

5 Heated suit and air-conditioned helmet with scratchproof visor.

6 Special tires allow a short trip to a garage even when punctured.

7 Catalytic converter reduces exhaust pollution.

8 Computerized engine operates at top efficiency.

9 Fuel stored at sides, so "fuel tank" can be used to store a helmet.

10 Metal-framed bodywork protects rider from side impacts.

Superbike Century

The best superbikes combine high power with good brakes and superb handling. These features enable a skilled rider to go fast, but safely. Acceleration is more important than top speed, so that other vehicles can be overtaken quickly.

◁ **FN Four** The 1905 Belgian FN Four was the world's first four-cylinder motorcycle. It also had shaft drive, another first. The model shown here is a 1921 750.

▽ **BMW R32** The first BMW was shown at the Paris motorcycle show of 1923. The sleek machine had a twin cylinder engine and shaft drive, which is featured on every BMW made.

△ **Zundapp K800** This 1932 machine had a pressed steel frame rather than the usual welded tubes. The last K800 was made in 1941, but the frame formed the basis of the KS750 sidecar outfit used by the German Army in World War II.

▷ **Ariel Square Four** First launched in 1931, the Square Four continued to be made until 1958. The engine was powerful but compact, with four cylinders arranged in a square. Note the "fishtail" exhaust on this 1937 model, a popular style of the time. Today's fashionable exhaust is shaped like a tin can, designed to look like the exhausts on racing bikes.

▷ **Vincent Black Shadow**
With a top speed of 200 km/h (125 mph) the Black Shadow was among the fastest bikes of the 1950s.

▽ **Honda CB750** The 1968 CB750 spearheaded Honda's drive into the superbike markets which were dominated by European and American makers. The bike had a smooth-as-silk engine, rocketship performance and good fuel economy.

▽ **Ducati 900SS** This Italian bike's low weight and stiff frame helped make it one of the best handling machines of the late 1970s.

◁ **Kawasaki ZX-10** Ridden on a test track at 268 km/h (167 mph), the ZX-10 was 1988's fastest road bike. The ZX-10's fairing keeps the wind off, while hooks fold out to keep small bags secure on the back of the saddle.

▷ **Suzuki NUDA** The NUDA is an idea for a near-future superbike. NUDA has two-wheel drive, with wheels and bodywork made of lightweight, but super-strong, carbon-fiber. The high seat and low handlebars make for an arm-stretching reach over the fuel tank.

27

Facts and records

Motorcycles have ranged from tiny, flying fleas to giant, overpowered monsters. The present range of superbikes is the most advanced ever, and here are some of the interesting developments that have led from slow and unreliable steamers to the high tech roadburners of the present.

Gottlieb Daimler patented his gasoline engined bicycle in 1885. In 1886, Wilhelm Maybach tested the machine. The tires were iron hoops fitted to wooden wheels, hardly high tech even in the Victorian age. Air-filled leather, canvas and rubber pneumatic tires had been tested on the Michelin brothers' experimental motor car in 1885, the year before the first motor cycle. There was an advantage to metal tires though. Early pneumatic tires were very fragile – iron was tough and reliable.

The first organized motorbike race was held in France in 1896. The course ran between the two cities of Paris and Nantes.

The first TT race was in 1907. The course, around the Isle of Man, is still the world's longest at 61 km (37.7 miles).

The first motor racetrack in the world was laid at Brooklands in Surrey, England. For many years, from 1909 until the site was closed in 1938, Brooklands was the center of British car and motorcycle racing.

Some designers of the 1920s and 1930s were obsessed with the idea of single wheeled bikes. In 1923, the magazine *Everyday Science* announced "a new terror of the road."

This was a large monowheel devised by E.J. Christie of the United States. He made a 4.6 m (14 ft) high model, and claimed that a roadgoing version, equipped with gyroscope and rudder, would go at 400 km/h (250 mph). There is no evidence that his machine was a success.

In 1929, A Rudge speedway bike was the first motorcycle to have some of its parts chrome plated. Today's Harley "hogs" and Honda Gold Wings are dripping with the shiny stuff.

German rider Ernst Henne was the fastest rider for 14 years as a result of his 1937 record of 279 km/h (173 mph).

The Harley-Davidson 45 WLA of World War II was equipped with a large holster for a submachine gun. Some 90,000 of these 738 cc V-twins were supplied to American and British troops.

Wilhelm Herz went into the record books when he hit 290 km/h

▽ Wilhelm Herz, aboard his NSU 500 speed bike.

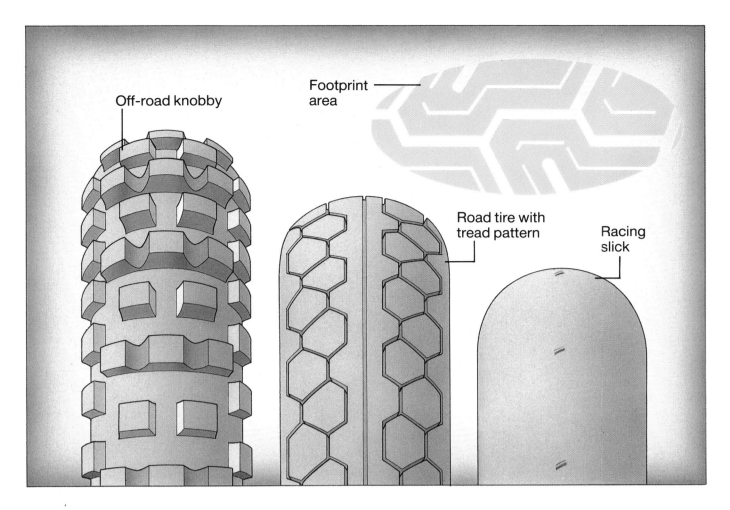

Off-road knobby

Footprint area

Road tire with tread pattern

Racing slick

(180 mph) on an NSU 500 in 1951. Before the record run, carried out on a German autobahn, his doctor advised him to strengthen his forearms so that he could keep control at high speed.
There were no trips to the gym for Wilhelm Herz though - he took up baking bread instead! Kneading the dough gave him the tough arm muscles he needed, as well as an enjoyable hobby that he continued for years afterwards.

Production of Japanese bikes numbered in just the hundreds in the late 1940s. Such was the success of the industry that in 1969, over 2.5 million bikes were made. In 1981 the figure had climbed to 7,412,582.

In 1979, Don Vesco was timed at 578 km/h (361 mph) on one part of the Bonneville course. Then a tire burst and Vesco crashed. He survived, but did not make another attempt.

On and off-road tires look different for good reasons. Off-road knobbies get grip in the dirt by sinking into and pushing against the surface. Street tires do the opposite – the rough asphalt or concrete digs into the smooth rubber. What we call a tread pattern is actually a number of grooves designed to channel water away. Racing "slicks" are entirely smooth tires, made for riding on dry circuits. By doing away with the tread, they offer the maximum amount of contact with the ground and so offer the most grip. The amount of tire touching the ground is called the "footprint area" – the bigger this contact patch, the better the grip.

When a tire is warmed up, it grips better. On a fast lap, the rear tire of a racing bike gets hotter than boiling water. 125°C (350°F) is common.

Since the beginning of the motorcycle industry more than 2000 different makes of motorcycle have been produced. Most firms were small, but many great names, such as Indian, BSA and Vincent went bust or have been taken over.

The Boccardo Aero 97 from France holds its fuel in plastic tanks on either side of the engine. What looks like a fuel tank is actually a storage compartment for a helmet.

Bike technology

This glossary explains many of the technical terms used in this book.

Antilock brake system (ABS)
This brake system prevents locked wheels in slippery conditions. In use, it feels like a vibrating pump action, felt through the brake levers, as the ABS briefly relaxes the brakes when they approach lock-up. ABS is particularly useful on a motorcycle, as a locked front wheel will flip bike and rider onto the ground instantly.

Bone shaker
Nickname given to early bicycles that had no springs or air-filled tires. The bumpy ride was literally bone shaking!

cc
Cubic centimeters. Describes the volume of an engine's cylinder. May be just 49 cc for a single-cylinder moped, 997 cc for a four-cylinder ZX-10. Cubic inches are sometimes used instead of cc.

Chain drive
Thick metal chain connecting gearbox to rear wheel. Needs regular oiling and adjustment to keep it at the correct tension. Needs replacing when it stretches too much. Used on most motorbikes, though some makers use shaft drive, especially suitable for tourers.

Customizing
Making a motorcycle a little different from others. Custom bikes often have chromed engine parts, a fat rear tire, long front forks and other additions. Most of the bigger bike manufacturers offer "factory customs" – bikes which have the customized look, but are bought ready to ride.

Cylinder
Central part of engine, in which a piston goes up and down. The piston is connected to a crankshaft, which changes the up-and-down motion to a smooth, rotating one. Bike cylinder arrangements are many and varied, ranging from single-

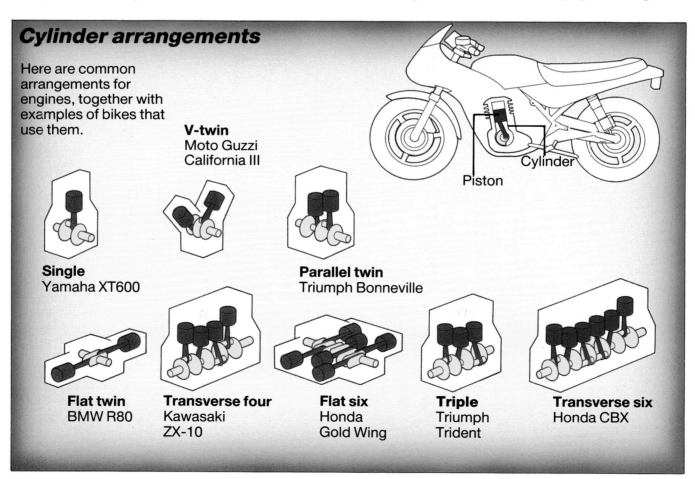

Cylinder arrangements

Here are common arrangements for engines, together with examples of bikes that use them.

V-twin
Moto Guzzi
California III

Cylinder

Piston

Single
Yamaha XT600

Parallel twin
Triumph Bonneville

Flat twin
BMW R80

Transverse four
Kawasaki
ZX-10

Flat six
Honda
Gold Wing

Triple
Triumph
Trident

Transverse six
Honda CBX

cylinder models to complex six-cylinder types. The diagram shows a range of such engines. Multi-cylinder engines are usually smoother, but singles or twins are simpler to maintain and can deliver their maximum power at slower engine speeds, so are good for off-road use where low-end power is more useful than sheer speed.

Fairing
Plastic bodywork designed to allow a bike to cut smoothly through the air and protect the rider from gale-force wind pressure.

Frame
Metal "backbone" that supports the engine and other parts of a bike.

Internal combustion (IC) engine
Engine in which fuel is burned inside the engine rather than, say, a steam engine in which fuel is burned outside a water-filled boiler to make steam.

Motorcycles use two main types of IC engine. The four-stroke system, similar to those used in automobiles, powers most bigger road machines. Racing and small sports bikes mostly use two-stroke power, shown here in the diagram. Its advantage is that more power is produced for its weight. Disadvantages include

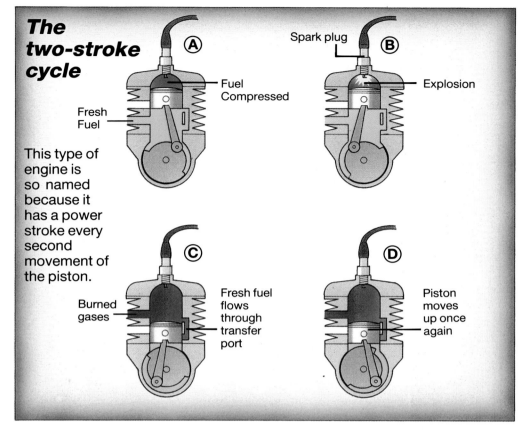

The two-stroke cycle

This type of engine is so named because it has a power stroke every second movement of the piston.

A — Fuel Compressed — Fresh Fuel

B — Spark plug — Explosion

C — Burned gases — Fresh fuel flows through transfer port

D — Piston moves up once again

poor fuel economy and pollution problems, as some fuel and oil go out with the burned exhaust gases.

The Ford Motor Company, with Australian engineer Ralph Sarich, is developing a new type of two-stroke engine with better fuel consumption and this may eventually be used on motorcycles.

Norton has turbine-smooth rotary engine bikes in limited production. These too may be developed more in the future.

Knobby
Name given to off-road tires that have a chunky tire section

MX
Short for motocross, the off-road motorcycle sport.

Outfit
Name given to motorcycle and sidecar. Also known as a combination.

Pillion
The name given to the rear seat of a motorcycle. Can be separate or simply the back of a long saddle.

Shaft drive
Rotating shaft, linking gearbox to rear wheel. Used especially by BMW, for all their bikes. Needs less attention than a chain.

Slick
Name given to the smooth racing tires

made for dry-weather use. They have no tread pattern. This pattern, cut into the rubber, is designed to channel water away from a tire when it is raining. The only marks on a slick are the tiny slots designed to show the depth of rubber in the tire.

Streamlining
Body-shaping to allow a bike to cut smoothly through the air. The best fairings direct the air away from a rider's body and over the helmet, leaving a calm area of air to sit in. Touring bikes often have big fairings. Sports models usually make do with small ones to cut down on weight.

Index

Ariel Square Four   26
Africa   12,23
Agostini, Giacomo   20
Albert of Belgium, King
                       15
Australia   22

Benz, Karl   9
BMW
    4,11,12,15,18,26,31
    KI   24
    R32   26
    R75   13
    R80   30
Boccardo Aero 97   29
Bonneville   29
Bonneville Salt Flats
                       11
Brooklands   28
Brough Superior   14
BSA   29
    Rocket III   4

Cannstatt   9
Christie, E.J.   28
Copeland, Lucius   6,7
Curtiss, Glenn
                 10,11,15

Daimler   10
    Gottlieb   9,28
    Paul   9
Davidson, Arthur   16
Daytona   15
Dixon, Freddie   17
Ducati 900SS   27

Europe   23
Everyday Science   28

Florida   10,15

FN Four   28
Ford Motor Company
                       31
France   13,28,29

Germany   14
Grand Prix   20,22

Harley-Davidson
                  16,17,30
    45 WLA   28
    Electra Glide   16
    "hog"   16,28
Harley, William   16
    Walter   16
Henderson   15
Henne, Ernst   11,28
Herz, Wilhelm   28
Hildebrand and
    Wolfmüller   9
Hildebrand, Heinrich
    and Wilhelm   9
Honda   18,19
    A-type   18
    CB750   18,27
    CBX   19,30
    Dream D-type   18
    Gold Wing   9,28,30

Indian   15,29
    Hendee Special   5
Isle of Man   18,20,28
Italy   20

Japan   18,24
Jeecy-Vea   15

Kawasaki   11,19
    Z1300   19
    ZX-10   27,30
    ZZR-1100   4

Lawrence of Arabia
                       14
Lightning Bolt   11

Maybach, Wilhelm
                  9,10,28
Megola   14
Michaux, Ernest and
    Pierre   6,7
    Cycle Club   7
Michelin brothers   28
Milwaukee   16
Moto Guzzi
    California III   17,30
Munich   9

Nantes   28
New York   7
Norton   13,31
NSU 500   28

Ormond Beach   10,11
Otto, Nikolaus   9

Paris   6,26,28
Paris-Dakar rally   23
Powa El-Tox   24

Rolls-Royce   14
Rudge speedway bike
                       28
Russia   12

Sarich, Ralph   31
Scott   15
St Germain-en-Laye   6
Surrey   28
Suzuki   19
    NUDA   27
    RG500   30

Tourist Trophy   18,20
Triumph   18
    Bonneville   30
    Trident   4,30
TT race   28

United States 11,15,16
Utah   11

Velocette   15
    Thruxton racer   15
Vesco, Donald   11,29
Vincent   29
    Black Shadow
                       27,29
von Saubronne-Davis
    velocipede   7

Walker, Ernie   15
Werner brothers   4
Werner motorcycle   9
World War I   12,13,14
World War II
                  12,13,26,28
Wolfmüller, Alois   9
Wynn's Safari   22

Yamaha OW01
    FZR 750R   5
    Virago   17
    XT600   30

Zundapp   12
    K800   26
    KS750   26

PRINTED IN BELGIUM BY

proost
INTERNATIONAL BOOK PRODUCTION